I0164153

DESIGNED TO DREAM

Rodney

Davis

Contents

ACKNOWLEDGEMENTS

I wish to give all glory to God for the thirst He has placed in me, and the desire He has given me to follow after Him. I further thank God every day for the extraordinary support and joy he has placed in my life, without which I could do so much less.

My wife, my perfect gift from God, backs me up, holds me up, and pushes me forward. She is always there, ready to serve and answer any call. I am respected in my home and at the city gates due in part to my virtuous wife.

My children and grandson: La Shelle, Jenna, Adonijah, Leah, Eden, Micah, and Joshua are an unending source of joy and pride! They amaze me every day with their differences, strengths, and determination.

I thank my parents-Shirley and Lonzo, my extended family, especially my aunts and uncles, and my Transformation Church family for their vigilant support in abiding with me on this journey.

Lastly, I would like to thank the editors for making sure that what I have to say is clear and concise and hits its mark!

This Only Happens in Movies

Clouds abound in the sky and rain pelts the windshield. Swish, swoosh, swish, swoosh, swoosh, swoosh… Horns are blaring. Sirens scream. On the horizon, the Delaware Memorial Bridge looms. The car is being pushed around by the wind. As I prepared to tell her the unbelievable story, I was dreading the evening. The weather conditions seemed to match the short words that came out of my mouth.

I repositioned the chair in the passenger seat of the car straight up from its normal comfortable spot; nervously, I put my hands on my knees, took a deep breath, and tried but failed to swallow. That's when the storm got the better of me, distorting my vision. Raindrops on the windshield seemed to form smiley faces, as if smiling at me. "Shame on you!" the wipers seemed to be saying as they shook their blades at me.

And the worship songs on the radio seemed to mock my life. I switched on the radio just in time to hear Kierra Sheard sing "You Don't Know" to my wife on the radio. Then Paul S. Morton began singing "Let It Rain" to the weather. Even TD

Jakes' single, "Take My Life," ministered suicide to me. I had come to the conclusion that I was being targeted on all sides, including the elements, and that my car was on my tail. You'd think I'd be able to recover my composure and see the bright side of things, realizing that it was only by God's grace that I was able to learn about my daughter.

It should have been easy to turn my sudden sadness into dancing once more. After all, I am a Christian and a member of God's Kingdom's Elder Council. All would always work out for the good of all who love the Lord, I knew. But I couldn't take my eyes off the smiley-face raindrops, who were smiling at me like little hyenas, and the wiper blades, who were shaking their heads as if they were superior to me.

Rainstorms have a way of making it seem more complicated. It's true what they say; when it rains, it pours. Bills pile up, family members behave irrationally, and friends turn against you. And then there are the roads. The roads, oh my goodness. Deadly crossroads, byroads, having to take the high road all the time, guilty low roads, feeling bad about inroads, railroads, gravel roads, frustrating roadblocks, difficult roadmaps, roadkill, and roadwork road rage, dead-end roads, and even back-stabbing roadies. What about the less-traveled paths?

Who can praise God on those roads of taking responsibility and accountability no matter how difficult the situation, admitting to adulterous affairs and broken commitments, admitting to a lack of honesty in financial matters, admitting that you are still addicted to alcohol and drugs like power, sex, and money?

Most of us believe we can't ... but are we really unable or is it that we just won't? We can do all this through Christ who strengthens us, according to God's Word. It also says, "In a spirit of heaviness put on a garment of praise." You want me to thank you and I'm feeling heavy right now? Maybe I should thank you if I had to tell her I was getting a promotion.

It is admirable to be able to move into a dream house. An all-expenses-paid vacation ... a new Mercedes-Benz ... being financially fortunate to do what I love ... all of these things will cause praise to pour freely from my mouth. Yet applaud you "in the midst of adversity"? The most intense moments are included in heaviness. A hard conversation about divorce, a heavy heart like when a loved one passes away, and a heavy burden of guilt when you have discovered you are the father of a child by another woman.

The last one stripped my skin and lips of moisture. As I approached the bridge, I spoke those memorable sentences. "I recently discovered that I am the father of an eleven-year-old child." It was right there in the open. Those terms were no longer looming in the back of my mind. I completed the task. I chose to take the high road. That wasn't so bad, was it? My doubts had been vanquished! For a brief moment at least...

My spirit was patting my flesh on the back for a job well done when I noticed the car swerving to the right as it lost full control while driving over the bridge. We were about to drive off the edge of the bridge. It seemed to be over to me. My life whizzed by in front of my eyes. "What are you doing?" I screamed. In an effort to locate her, I yelled her name. In out-of-control circumstances, I usually scream out the word above all names—Jesus—but it didn't come out first this time. I believe it did come out a split second later. My admission was entirely necessary. My admission was appropriate. Her answer, on the other hand, made me uneasy.

We were both perplexed and disoriented by this situation at this stage. My wife pulled over after barely making it over the bridge so I could take the wheel and safely drive us home. I was so irritated by the situation that I missed exit after exit on a drive that was supposed to be a straight shot home. The more I drove the more I felt like a leading man in a Hollywood movie.

After passing through city after city, I kept saying, "This sort of thing just happens in movies." *Tyler Perry should do something about this farrago,* I thought as we pulled over to a gas station. We walked away from the gas station. I wondered how I could contact Maurie Povich because this circumstance could not possibly be true. Then, because of the silence, I flipped back on the radio to hear William Murphy sing that song. *"I vow to praise you in the good and in the bad. If you're happy or sad, I'll praise you. I'll praise you whether happy or sad. I'll praise you in all that I go through because praise is what I do. I owe it all to you."* What a wonderful tune! Those words echoed loud in my ears in the midst of my deepest sorrow. They slashed me like a two-edged sword. If David could bless You at all times for what he had to deal with, I might stop feeling sorry for myself and say thank you.

Instead of continuing my pity party, I started to see this as a blessing rather than a curse. God intended for me to find out right now. She must need my assistance. I was in desperate need of her. This time was predetermined by God. God is aware of the situation. I am surrounded by God. He has the final say. I began to thank and worship Him for helping me to find out with renewed courage. In my eyes, the storm had become nothing more than a soft drizzle as a result of this latest revelation.

That day, I realized that, while we can't control the wind and waves or the storms that come our way, we can control how we respond to them; we can skillfully navigate through them by the ability God has given to us. I recalled how the disciples had to endure a similar ordeal. Replace the blue Ford Expedition with a big fishing boat, the Delaware Memorial Bridge with the Galilean Sea, and heavy rains with strong winds and you've got yourself a similar scenario.

"He could see they were in big trouble, rowing hard and fighting the wind and waves. Jesus approached them about three o'clock in the morning, walking on the river. He planned to go around them..." The Sea of Galilee is located at a depth of 680 feet below sea level. It is surrounded by hills that rise to a height of up to 2000 feet with an exceptionally dry and cool climate. The atmosphere around the sea, on the other hand, is warm and humid.

The pressure and temperatures change abruptly as a result of this significant temperature differential. This transition has resulted in strong winds spiraling into the sea. Since the Sea of Galilee is small, these strong winds generate raging waves, resulting in a sudden and violent storm that could last up to three days. The astute disciples realized they were in big trouble. What should have been a simple ride turned into a bumpy ride. They resembled a tossed and guided ship with no sail. Like smoke, the clear vision vanished.

The sailors were subjected to a coup d'état by the winds. The unwary boat was tossed about by the winds and waves. The disciples toiled against the storm for a long time, panicked. They pushed on, determined to get to the other side, but the storm was much too strong. They had no idea that Jesus had seen them straining from afar. Perhaps we, too, are unaware of this fact. And if we can't see Jesus, he can see us!

The miracle of Jesus coming to the disciples walking on the water was much more incredible than Jesus seeing them struggle in the middle of the sea.

And if we are unable to reach Jesus, he will still reach us! They couldn't believe what they were seeing. Quite literally! "It's a ghost!" They were in tears. Who'd have guessed that Jesus would be moonwalking on the water? I'm not one of them! The disciples didn't either. This level of understanding Jesus had not yet been reached. We want God to come to us in the same way He has in the past. During praise and worship times during Sunday services or prayer times for shut-ins, we look forward to His arrival.

In our revivals, miracle crusades, and Power of God conventions, we search for God. Do we, on the other hand, look for Him in death, divorce, illness, and depression? If God is the God of the elements, He must also be the God of life's storms. In our limitations, His power is mastered or at its peak. God will frequently allow difficult circumstances to occur so that He may show Himself to us in a new light. Effortful moments also humble us and remind us of our complete reliance on God.

In a way, as Jesus walked on water, he was demonstrating to the disciples that he was in control of the storm that had them out of control. God has the final say. That is what He desires for us to understand. He's in the midst of your horrific hurricane. He's jaywalking on the water of the crisis. On the water of the setbacks, God is sleepwalking. He is cross-walking on your sickness' water. God is the nightwalker when life becomes bleak, grim, and gloomy. To Him, our problems are nothing more than a walk in the park.

Since going through a lot of these challenges, I've discovered that the biggest storms make the best stories. Looking back on my high school and college years, I see that I made many errors. When I should have stood my ground, I caved in to peer pressure, lied when I should have told the truth, reacted when I should have responded, clung to friendships when I should have let go, and followed when I should have led. I wanted vengeance. I played games; I didn't research; I stayed up too late; I broke hearts; I indulged; I lusted after the flesh; I loved and trusted the wrong people.

I'd made a lot of mistakes and was sure to make a lot more before I changed my mind one day. Since I was not where I wanted to be, regretting what I had done in the past was crippling my current realities and weakening my potential. In my view, I was giving my past a penthouse apartment. My mind started to realize that past errors no longer existed, except in the places where I had allowed them to exist. I learned right away that the mistakes I'd made were already part of God's master plan for my life.

Rollover minutes on a mobile phone aren't as good as God's mercies. Every day, they are transformed into something different. Yes, there were times when I felt as though I had used up all of the mercies that had been set aside for me. There was no reason to be concerned because the next day would bring new mercies. Accepting this reality is so refreshing, not to take advantage of it but to welcome it. I learned a valuable lesson from Ishmael's story.

He was born as a result of Abraham and Sarah's error. His name means God hears. He was the oldest child, but he was not a promising son. He was a bondslave's wife. His mother was a concubine and a maidservant. He was a rejected child. Family and community had turned their backs on him. His father had abandoned him, but God saved him. Why did God intervene to save him? For purpose. Destiny is a powerful word. The abyss. The Ishmaelites were the ones who purchased Joseph and rescued him from the pit of death and misery.

Only God has the power to deliver a Joseph using an Ishmael. Only God can transform a blunder into a blessing. Only God can turn a tragedy into a triumph.

Maybe you're in a hole as well. The abyss of mistakes is depressing you and complicating your life. Like a dump, the pit of messes is filling up. Your life has a cavity due to the pitiful remorse of bad choices and decisions. Engage your feelings with God's word of revelation. God has the ability to mature you in your mess and turn you into one of the best ministers on the planet by learning from your mistakes.

And when the odds are stacked against you, you will conquer them. Know that God's grace is sufficient to remove even the most stubborn stains. Seek His forgiveness on a regular basis. Then forgive yourself for the mistakes you've made in the past because God has already done so. And when you want to hang on to your sins does God remember them? Forget about the past, and don't think about the past. Allow yourself to let go of the mistakes you've made as well as what others have done to you. God will make all things new (Micah 7:19; 2 Corinthians 5:17; Isaiah 43:18).

I saw my ministry collapse and my testimony become untrustworthy through shameful eyes. Respect for me as a man of God was eroding. The state of my reputation deteriorated. All who were once by my side turned against me. My wife left me. My employer terminated my employment. I saw myself as being lower than what my rivals thought of me through shameful eyes. I was a grasshopper in my own eyes. Hearing rumors, I assumed someone was saying negative things about me. In the gossiper's mouth, I had become the main topic, the main subject of debate in the church.

Preachers need fuel in the pulpit; for the stand-up comic, new material is available. In the barbershop, there was a loud laugh. I was the topic of discussion in the beauty store. I was the talk of the town when I heard whispers. Feeling extremely emotional, I became bitter, dispirited, and disillusioned. I wanted to get away from it all. To get out of it, I was lying. To make me feel better, I was blaming. I felt hemmed in. I was at a loss for words, wasn't sure where to go. Nobody would be able to understand.

Nothing was important anymore. I was deeply emotional and felt completely alone. Then God showed me nakedness through ashamed eyes. Unbridled lust. An affair. Pregnancy. The plot. A man's demise. A child being conceived in sin. The death of the child. Night-long laments from a father for his child. Shrill cries. Judgement. Hurt. Pain.

I see, hear, and feel something else with ashamed eyes, whispered words, and feeling intensely emotional. "I've transgressed against the Lord." (12:13a) (2 Samuel 12:13a) There will be no shifting of blame. There will be no denial. There are no justifications. There will be no double-talk. I overheard a sin confession. An acknowledgment of responsibility. One man being open and frank about his sin. Repentance is a state of mind. I saw a man who was a man after God's own heart. He considers you to be the apple of His eye.

I had a sense of forgiveness. Restorative work. *"The Lord has also taken away your sin; you shall not die," Nathan told David* (2 Samuel 12:13b). David and Bathsheba were the couple in question. But David was the one who took over. He took responsibility for his actions. He was solely responsible for the situation. He replied with a divinely inspired solution. "Behold, I was born in iniquity, and my mother conceived me in sin. You seek truth in your innermost being, and you will reveal wisdom to me in the secret portion. I'll be clean if you purify me with hyssop. Wash me, and I shall be whiter than snow.

"Make me hear joy and gladness, Let the bones which You have broken rejoice. Hide Your face from my sins And blot out all my iniquities. Create in me a clean heart, O God, And renew a steadfast spirit within me. Do not cast me away from Your presence And do not take Your Holy Spirit from me. Restore to me the joy of Your salvation And sustain me with a willing spirit." With passive people overlooking David's flaws, he would never take the burden. If Nathan hadn't been speaking in parables and had told David about a true thief, David would have killed him and gone on with his wrongdoings.

David would not have come to a position of repentance, in my opinion. Confrontations force us to make fast, long-term decisions. David made a brilliant decision about perhaps one of the most important moments of his life. He did something that no other king had ever done before. He admitted it, believed it, confessed it, and repented of it. God pardoned him, but he was still held accountable for the seeds he had sown.

Even then, God's grace was appropriate for David. The plot then progresses to the crux of the problem: how to return after being convicted. "Then David rose from the earth, washed, anointed himself, changed his apparel, and went into the house of the Lord to worship; then he returned to his own house, and they set bread before him, and he ate." (2 Samuel 12:20) His attention was drawn to a wall of whisperers. He passed by the worst-case scenario in his mind. A hypothetical question was posed by him. They reluctantly said yes, expecting David to hurt himself. What do you do if God does not provide you with the response you seek?

CHAPTER 1

WHAT IS A DREAM?

Have you ever felt a peculiar feeling on your skin when you first wake up?

The sensation of being a part of another world, or, to put it another way, of what is commonly referred to as "a dream"? The response is self-evident: we can all claim to have dreamed. But what exactly is a dream?

This dream vision can include any images, feelings, or emotions that you have while sleeping. Dreams can be extremely simple or extremely hazy; they can be full of joyful memories or terrifying sensations; they can be understandable or illogical and perplexing. Many people have wondered and continue to wonder. Many people have been intrigued by it over the years, and it continues to fascinate them. The dream, for example, portrays a fortunate moment for the ancient Greeks, a moment of contact between man and God.

However, for many of us the dream remains an unknown, the huge question mark that we know contains images, feelings, and emotions that are formed and experienced while we sleep. A divine dream is a dream that God gives to man when he sleeps in some circumstances. Since it's a dream, you can only get it while you're sleeping. When you're alive, you don't have any 'daydreams.' When alive, one can only receive dreams, as we will see later; or, if God so desires, one can hear a divine voice speaking audibly without seeing anything, so to speak, as often happened to the ancient prophets of God who heard the voice of God speak to them while they were fully awake and without any vision.

We are confronted with a discovery in this situation. However, I'd like to point out that a revelation can also be obtained in a dream or vision, according to Scripture.

Let's return to dreams. Every human being dreams while sleeping, and among the dreams he has, there may be those that are from God. I say "may" because it all depends on God.

Abraham fell into a deep slumber during which God foretold that his descendants would live as strangers in a land that was not theirs for four hundred years and that God would judge the nation to which they were slaves and determine whether they would leave with great riches (Gen. 15: 12–16). God appeared to King Abimelech in a dream at night and told him that the woman he had taken, Sarah, had a husband and that he had to return her to Abraham or he would die with his entire household (Genesis 20:1–7).

On his way to Charan, Jacob had a dream in which he saw a ladder resting on the ground, the top of which reached the sky, and God's angels ascending and descending the ladder, and then God spoke to him (Gen. 28: 10–22). While serving Laban, Jacob had a dream in which God revealed to him that he had seen what Laban had done to him and that he should return to his homeland (Gen. 31: 10–13). In a dream, God appeared to Laban as he pursued Jacob, telling him not to talk to him for good or evil (cf. Gen. 31: 22–25).

Joseph, Jacob's uncle, had dreams in which God predicted that one day his brothers would bow down before him (Gen. 37: 5–11).

When Joseph was in prison in Egypt, the chief of the cupbearers and the chief of the bakers, who had been imprisoned for wrongdoing against Pharaoh, both had dreams on the same night, one for each, in which God foretold what would happen to them in three days. These dreams were interpreted by Joseph, and things happened according to his interpretation (Gen. 40: 1–22).

When Joseph was in prison, Pharaoh had two visions in which God foretold him seven years of prosperity and seven years of famine; these dreams were also interpreted by Joseph, whom Pharaoh took out of prison to interpret these dreams (Gen. 41: 1–36). When Gideon was about to collapse on the field of Midian during the time of the Judges, God ordered him to go down to the field of Midian and listen to what they were saying.

He did as he was told, and when he arrived at the camp, he overheard a man telling his companion about a dream he had the night before, in which he saw bread all around him, of barley rolling into the camp of Midian, It hit the tent and the tent flipped over and fell to the ground. This barley loaf, according to the interpretation given by the companion, was the sword of Gideon to whom God had given Midian and the whole field. This dream was a confirmation to Gideon that God had given him the field of Midian and strengthened his hands (Judg. 7: 9–18).

God appeared to King Solomon in a dream and asked him to ask Him for what he desired, and Solomon asked for a wise heart (1 Kings 3: 4–15).

Daniel interpreted a dream that Nebuchadnezzar, King of Babylon, had in which God showed him the kingdoms that would come after him (Dan. 2: 1–49). This king still had a dream in which God showed him the punishment he would receive for being proud in his heart (Dan. 4: 1–37), which was also interpreted by Daniel.

Joseph, Mary's husband, had a dream just when he was about to secretly leave Mary (because she was pregnant), and in this dream an angel of the Lord appeared to him and told him not to worry about taking Mary as his wife because what she was begotten was by the Holy Spirit (Matt. 1: 18–25).

The wise men who came from the East, after finding the child Jesus and worshiping him, received a dream from God in which God told them not to go back to Herod (Matt. 2:12). Joseph had another dream in which an angel of the Lord told him to flee to Egypt with Mary and the child Jesus and to stay there until he told him to return to Israel (Matt. 2: 13–15).

Also, while Joseph was in Egypt, after Herod was dead, he received another dream in which an angel of the Lord ordered him to return to Israel (Matt. 2: 19–21). And once he returned to Israel, since Archelaus reigned in Judea instead of Herod, he was divinely warned in a dream and went to dwell in Galilee (Matt. 2: 22–23).

QUESTIONS

◆ Explain the word "DREAM"

_____

_____

_____

_____

_____

_____

_____

_____

◆ Is there a difference between DREAM and VISION?

_____

_____

_____

_____

_____

_____

_____

_____

_____

PRINCIPLE POINTS

◆ Dreams are impressions on the minds of sleeping persons, made by divine agency.

◆ A dream remains an unknown until it is interpreted.

CHAPTER 2

THE MAN AND HIS DREAM

I eventually decided to fulfill one of my dreams in 2007. My ambition was to create my own gospel stage show. In a dream, I was on stage, holding a microphone in front of thousands of people. The transition from me preaching on stage at a church service to welcoming the audience following the play production was unusual. My alarm clock woke me up as soon as I saw this.

This dream seemed so true to me. I couldn't believe it when I realized none of it was true; that I wasn't living the life of a dreamer. I wasn't exactly living the dream. I'd awoken to the same surroundings, the same dilapidated three-bedroom duplex; the same rowdy neighbors who would stay up all night drinking beer and shouting profanely as if everyone in the area was unemployed and had nowhere to go in the morning. I had a beat-up blue Ford Expedition and I had no idea whether it would start or not.

I was jolted awake by a harsh reality check. However, I did find that other things began to awaken inside me. New energy, new thoughts, the anointing, divine frustration, and passion were all part of my dream. I had to make a choice. I felt like David, the shepherd boy who asked the Lord, "Shall I pursue?"

"Is this dream from you or is it just self-ambition?" I prayed, seeking answers.

God did not communicate with me in a deep, majestic voice. He didn't answer in a quiet, small voice either. Nonetheless, He gave me an inner knowing that if He gave me the dream, I'd find a way to make it a reality. God will always provide for the vision that He gives man. That day, in the summer of 2007, I resolved not to treat the God-given dream like junk mail, discarding or deleting the very meaning and destiny God had for my life. I was not going to let my true abilities go unnoticed; instead, I was going to discover and explore my unique talent.

Do you have any doubts about whether or not your dream came from God? Have you ever handled your dreams as if they were junk mail? Is the scale of your dream a source of anxiety for you? Is there any resistance or opposition preventing you from following your dream? Do you have any idea where to start? Do you know how to make your vision a reality? Are you most afraid of pursuing the dream you most desire? This chapter is an empowerment session designed to help you unleash your inner dreamer!

"For God does speak—now one way, now another—though no one perceives it. In a dream, in a vision of the night, when deep sleep falls on people as they slumber in their beds..." (Job 33:14,15 NIV)

"His divine power has granted to us all things that pertain to life and godliness, through the knowledge of him who called us to his glory and excellence..." (II Peter 1:3 ESV)

"The secret things belong unto the LORD our God: but those things which are revealed belong unto us and to our children forever, that we may do all the words of this law." (Deuteronomy 29:29)

God talks to us, according to the book of Job, and one of the ways He speaks to us is through the medium of dreams. However, we are often unaware of this.

The explanations for this may be that our dreams are weird or creepy, or that they are full of symbols, or that they are in the form of parables. We ignore God's orders, miracles, and blessings because we don't recognize that our visions are from Him. Deuteronomy 29:29 tells us these dreams belong to us and our children. Dreams are our unseen seeds that we must plant and water in order for God to grow and create a tangible harvest through us.

If you don't recognize your dreams, you and your children will miss out on what God has already planned for you. Despite the fact that our dreams can seem irrational, they are a revelation from God to us. And this knowledge is all we need to carry out His will for our lives. We see God using visions to communicate with His people in the Bible. He used dreams to advise, guide, alert, prophesy blessing or imminent crisis, grant requests, and answer questions, among other things.

These dreams were sometimes bizarre, but they were genuine. God was and still is unconcerned with who He is dealing with. He addressed saints and sinners, kings and slaves, Israelites and Egyptians in His sermons. And He talked often. God continues to talk to us through dreams because He is the same yesterday, today, and forever. And if He was able to bring their dreams to fulfillment in the past, He can certainly bring our dreams to fruition if you are willing to follow them.

"If He did it before, He can do it again," someone said. The same God who exists today is the same God who existed in the past. Scripture also shows that He uses dreams to connect with His people and will continue to do so in the future. Acts chapter 2 says, "And it shall come to pass in the last days, saith God, I will pour out of my Spirit upon all flesh: and your sons and your daughters shall prophesy, and your young men shall see visions, and your old men shall dream dreams:" (Acts 2:17)

QUESTIONS

◆ Is there any resistance or opposition preventing you from
following your dream?

_____

_____

_____

_____

_____

_____

_____

◆ Do you have any idea where to start?

_____

_____

_____

_____

_____

_____

_____

_____

_____

_____

◆ Do you know how to make your dream a reality?

_____

_____

_____

_____

_____

_____

_____

_____

_____

PRINCIPLE POINTS

◆ If you don't recognize your dreams, you and your children
will miss out on what God has already planned for you.

◆ God continues to talk to us through dreams because He is the same yesterday, today, and forever.

◆ Your dream is your bearing to get to where God is taking you.

CHAPTER 3

THE GOD DREAM

Is My Dream from God?

The Bible is a surefire way to determine whether or not your dream is from God. The questions you should be asking yourself are, "Does my dream suit God's biblical principles?" "Is it possible for the Word to direct my dreams? Is there something in it that goes against it?" All we need for life, or everlasting life, and godliness, or living a godly life, has already been granted to us, according to 2 Peter 1:3.

What else could it be but God's infallible Word? The term "has" connotes the past tense. We already have everything we need to ensure that we are fulfilling God's dreams in our instruction manual. This raises an intriguing question. Many dreamers believe they need other people's consent, approval, or opinions in order to achieve their goals. Other dreamers feel that they must be at ease in order to pursue their goals. Some dreamers assume that their fantasies must be rational.

Even so, there are more dreamers who feel that in order to achieve their goals they must have the right circumstances. These ideas are not supported by the Bible in any way.

DREAMS AND ADVICE

Do I Need Anyone's Opinion?

Seeking guidance from people to whom God has not given the dream is one of the worst things you can do after receiving a dream from God. He would have given them the dream if He wanted them to have an opinion on it. Allowing people to keep you asleep because they haven't dreamed your dream or don't understand what you dreamed is not a good idea. Go after the dream that God has given you!

What happens is that we share our dream with a pessimist or a sceptic who is loaded with skepticism and mistrust. A chicken who is terrified of venturing into deep water. An elderly dog who is set in his ways and hasn't dreamed in a long time. Or, worst of all, a hater who secretly wants to see you lose and thinks they've been summoned only for this moment to stab you in the back. Allowing a negative speaker to have a commanding voice in your ear is never a good idea. "However," you object, "what about Pharaoh and how he tried Joseph's guidance and interpretation?" That's a good idea. Please allow me to explain some advice.

It must never be your goal to get someone's opinion on what God has revealed to you as you seek advice. What you want to do is search out advisors or leaders who are more prolific or knowledgeable about the Bible than you are and ask if your dream is consistent with the Bible. Pharaoh was not in tune with God or His Word, so he needed someone who was and who could interpret his dream. Like Pharoah, make sure you go to someone who is more scripturally sound with the Word and interpretation, and who has God's spirit.

DREAMS AND PEACE

Why Is There So Much Opposition?

"It doesn't bother me. That confirms that this dream came from God!" That's not the case. Having inner peace regarding a situation is highly subjective and entirely dependent on your viewpoint. You may be at ease about it because you lack a thorough understanding of God's Word; as a result, even if anything goes against what the Bible says, you won't feel guilty about it. Another reason you might be at ease is that your inner senses of right and wrong have become so numb that doing wrong no longer bothers you.

Wrong appears to be right and right appears to be wrong. You cannot use having inner peace about pursuing your desires as a criterion. The question you must ask yourself is, "Does pursuing my dream foster peace in my community?" Inner peace isn't enough to make you want to fulfill your dream. Nonetheless, you must be aware that, though your dream promotes peace and prosperity, there will always be those who oppose and fight it. Nonetheless, opposition and resistance are important markers for you. They act as a guide to the door God has opened for you. 1 Corinthians 16:9 says, "For a great door and effectual is opened unto me, and there are many adversaries." (KJV)

Adversaries opposing you and your dream are simply signs that you are on the right track. Enemies always put up the most resistance right at the beginning or end of your dreams. You must, however, make up your mind that you will not be defeated. Make the decision right now.

DREAMS AND UNEXPECTED OPPRESSORS

What Do I Do When Those That Are Closest Turn on Me?

When I decided to follow a big dream of mine not long ago, I was totally taken aback by some of the people who turned out to be my foes. I'd always expected to run into adversaries who didn't want everyone but themselves to succeed. These individuals are unmistakably haters. They're easy to spot from a mile away. They are perpetually pessimistic. They will often join committees to inform you of all the reasons why it cannot be achieved. Alternatively, they will inform you of all the dangers in order to make you fearful of following your dream.

Some adversaries will openly stand in your way, preventing you from fulfilling your mission and calling. But never in a million years did I imagine that some of my best friends would become my fiercest foes. I couldn't imagine that my mentors, instructors, and pastors would become my greatest adversaries. In this case, what was I supposed to do? Could I pay attention? Could I follow their advice like I had in the past? Should I stifle what I knew? Or should I stay away from them? Why didn't I turn around and leave? Was it possible to go around them? Would it have been better if I just skipped them?

Rodney Louis Davis is my name.

In fact, I'm just a regular guy with extraordinary ambitions. In comparison to most men, I am average height at six foot one inch. Yet I never imagined that any of my best friends would become my fiercest foes. I couldn't believe my mentors, coaches, and pastors would be my greatest foes. I didn't know what to do in this case.

Do I have to pay attention? Can I, as in the past, respect their advice? Do I stifle my knowledge? Is it better to stay away from them? Retrace my steps? Is it possible to skirt them? Is it better if I just skip over them?

Rodney Louis Davis is my real name. In fact, I'm just a regular guy with big dreams. In comparison to most men, I am about six foot one inch tall. I was attending to God's business. "If you delight yourself in the Lord, He will grant you your heart's desires." Is that correct? God brought a play I'd been working on for a long time to completion.

I told a pastor about it. I told him that I did not want the credit. It was possible that it would come under his purview. He sat on it for two months and didn't say anything. Perhaps it wasn't good enough, I reasoned. Perhaps it missed a lot of stuff. I had no idea. All I knew was that I was the one who penned the vision. I made it easy. I was certain that God had put people in position to carry it out. I assumed the runner would be the priest. But that wasn't the case. Other people who read the vision and believed it were used by God. I went ahead and did it.

I figured the pastor would be pleased with me. *Please back me up. Be my number one fan, just like a father does for his son. Please join me in my corner. Push me a little bit more.* This, however, did not occur. He became my number one competitor the week after my debut of *When It Rains.* An opponent. The brethren's accuser. Any time he took a step closer to realizing his dream, he felt threatened. He interpreted it as me attempting to compete in the same market as him. I saw it as a way of doing ministry in the arts. He objected.

He convened a church conference of about 30 "yes" representatives to oppose me. It was to inform me that it was not my season. It wasn't the right time for me. It was incorrect. It was carried out in complete secrecy. It got in the way of other things that were already happening. He admitted to the others that he was unaware of the play. He was out to get me. This betrayal was one of the most traumatic things I'd ever gone through. Despite being shocked, shaken, and embarrassed, I regrouped and continued on my path.

Maybe you're in the same boat as me. Your closest friends and family have humiliated and betrayed you. Those you expected to love, help, and encourage you are not there. Allowing strangers to hold you awake because they haven't dreamed your dream is not a good idea because they don't understand what you dreamed. Go after the dream GOD has awakened in you! My joy never faded. I debuted my play with a huge smile, bruised and beaten.

It was only a few people short of being sold out. I walked onto the stage at the end of the performance, tears in my eyes, one arm extended, pointing to heaven, and saying, "Thank you, Lord." A standing ovation welcomed me with a warm embrace. After that, someone came onto the stage and handed me red roses and a yellow star-shaped balloon. Since the balloon fell off the string and went up into the sky, it was a memorable moment for me.

The next thing out of my mouth was, "I think God is telling me I'm a rising star." What a once-in-a-lifetime opportunity. *The majority of playwrights never have this opportunity,* I pondered. *Most playwrights probably haven't been through what I went through to get here either,* I reasoned in the back of my mind.

When I was insulted and threatened, how did I keep my cool? I've discovered that dream killers exist not only in the universe but also in our congregations of churches; not only the people with whom you serve but also the people with whom you live. It's one thing to be attacked by people who have previously shown similar habits, but it's another to be attacked by people you call brothers, sisters, parents, politicians, and pastors. These are the people trust to love, encourage, identify, bless, train, nurture, direct, and treat us delicately. You don't have to put on a play to become the center of attention and the subject of any church gossip.

Just look at the graves of geniuses who perished while sharing their vision with skeptics. Committees formed solely to come up with millions of ways the revolutionary ideas can't perform, rather than to accomplish a mission. Or the entrepreneur to whom you expressed your vision in the hopes of forming a partnership instead took it and created it on their own. They are dream assassins. The divorced girlfriend, the inebriated driver, the tsunami, and the earthquake.

When your dream suddenly takes a detour, how do you get back on the road? When your spirit woefully weighs you down, how do you exercise the strength to muscle your way back into the race?

DREAMS AND DETOURS

Are Detours from God or Satan?

Jacob's son Joseph. God will increase him, as his name implies. When he receives a dream from God, he is just a young 17-year-old teenager. He should be unimportant since he is almost the last of Jacob's 12 sons to be born. But don't be fooled by his age or birth order. His birth order is unimportant, but his dream is more important than Pharaoh's palace! That's where he rose to become Egypt's second-in-command.

Don't be put off by the scale of your dream! Don't be afraid to do what you really want to do in life. Isn't it odd that the scale of your dream is about to annoy your family members?

Joseph had a simple life ahead of him. Since he was the firstborn of Jacob's caring wife Rachel, he was his father's favorite. When his half-brothers nearly killed him, he had just been given a nice coat and a dream. Joseph was assaulted and thrown into a pit by envious and despising half-brothers from Jacob's first wife, Leah, who were jealous of Joseph's dream and his father's favor.

Joseph never gave up despite being battered and broken. He stuck to his plan. He lost his father, his family, his house, and his coat in the process. Old dominance is threatened by dangerous dreamers! Joseph, on the other hand, never gave up on his dream. This naive, spoiled adolescent grew into a mature, big-hearted Hebrew leader in Egypt. "You meant it for evil, but God meant it for my good!" he explained to his brothers, who had come to Egypt begging because of the drought, after being crowned as Pharaoh's second-in-command in all of Egypt.

Your dream detour is about to put you in front of great people and lead you to the place God has had planned for you all along. Joseph was never grumpy. He realized that it was God who sent him to Egypt, not his brothers, in order to save his life and the lives of his family. I'm currently researching Joseph's story. I'm curious as to how he managed to maintain such a positive outlook. In our families, half-brothers still prey. In our temples, for example. You don't have to be your father's favorite to go from having exclusive dresses, apartments, and money to having none.

Just ask the woman whose sister passed away from cancer. Parents who are waiting for military special ops units to locate their child's remains, for example. The wife whose husband dies suddenly, the foster child who has been abandoned by their parents, and the soldier whose leg is blown off. The mother of a young boy who was shot because he was wearing a hoodie. Dreams have been cataclysmically rerouted. What's the best way to get back on track?

Let's look at Joseph again for a few more pointers. Take a look at how he's dressed. Look through the peephole in the Egyptian prison's wall. He's shackled. Is it the young, attractive man with the athletic build? That's Joseph, the man who had a divine dream. He's fallen into yet another abyss. There are guards this time. He's probably scratching his head, trying to figure out how all of this fits into his dream.

If God gave you a dream, you must find a way to make it a reality! The main road was detoured. Potiphar's house was the source of the new trouble. Despite Joseph's best efforts to flee Potiphar's wife, she accused him of attempting to rape her. He was imprisoned in an erroneous manner. Joseph's dream made it across a pit only to be imprisoned. It made it through a jail that was supposed to train him for the palace where his dream would come true. Potiphar's wife slandered and defamed his reputation. But the Lord was with Joseph also in prison.

He was treated with kindness and had favor with the warden. He was given command of the entire prison by the warden. Joseph was successful in everything he did because of the Lord. Joseph's detour to his dream landed him in a situation he never would have wanted for himself. His detour, however, became his tour of duty in the pursuit of his destiny and the realization of his God-sized dream.

There's a distinction to be made between distractions and detours. A distraction is something that stops you from fully immersing yourself in your dream. A detour, on the other hand, is a path built to get you to the same destination when the normal route is unavailable. Satan is the source of distractions. Satan is out to stop you from achieving your goals. God sends us detours. He wants to make sure you get your promise, so He'll make a way where there isn't one.

Your detour is about to put you in front of great people and lead you to the place God has had planned for you all along!

QUESTIONS

◆ Does my dream suit God's biblical principles?

_____

_____

_____

_____

_____

_____

_____

_____

_____

_____

◆ Is it possible for the Word to direct my dreams?

_____

_____

_____

_____

_____

_____

_____

_____

_____

_____

PRINCIPLE POINTS

◆ The Bible is a surefire way to determine whether or not your dream is from God.

◆ Seeking guidance from people to whom God has not given the dream is one of the worst things you can do after receiving a dream from God.

◆ Don't be put off by the scale of your dream!

◆ If God gave you a dream, you must find a way to make it a reality!

CHAPTER 4

DREAMS AND DIRECTION

"I will stand upon my watch, and set me upon the tower, and will watch to see what he will say unto me, and what I shall answer when I am reproved.

"And the Lord answered me, and said, Write the vision, and make it plain upon tables, that he may run that readeth it.

"For the vision is yet for an appointed time, but at the end, it shall speak, and not lie: though it tarry, wait for it; because it will surely come, it will not tarry." (Habakkuk 2:1–3)

When God talks to us through dreams, we must do some work in order to be led by a clear vision. Symbols, forms, mysterious objects, locations, and other things are often connected with God speaking to us in dreams. A simple vision guided every great leader in the Bible. If they were confused about their dreams, they sought explanation and guidance on how to make sense of them. If you and I are going to bring the dream to life inside of us, we must first get our vision straight.

"I will ... wait and see what he will say unto me..." Habakkuk said.

We usually use our ears to hear what someone is saying when they talk. Habakkuk says, "watch to see what he will say." The revelation is this: when God talks to us, we must translate what He is saying into something we can picture. Have you ever heard anyone say something like, "See what I'm saying?" That's where it originates.

We need to visualize what God is saying. As a result, we must first hear and then see it. We must then write it down after we have visualized it. Habakkuk then says, "Write the vision, and make it plain..."

First – we must hear it.

Second – we must see it.

Third – we must write it down (so that not only you but others can understand it and be directed by your dream).

That's right! Others are going to believe in your dream. God has already assembled a group of people with unique characteristics that are ideal for the dreams He wants you to realize. It's worth noting that Habakkuk said, "That he can run who reads it." You, not by yourself but as part of a community. Every vision that God gives will be accompanied by provision. It is our responsibility to hear it, see it, write it down, proclaim it, and believe it.

It is God's responsibility to provide us with a team to assist us in bringing forth the dreamer within us. Many people who stepped out on faith to follow God-given dreams often end up in barren wombs, a place of failure, unfruitfulness, and hopelessness. Barren wombs are people who have given up on their dreams and are just walking through their destinies. These people reached a point where they started to discount and dismiss the significance of their dreams.

Dealing with one setback after another, as well as taking huge risks that only resulted in major setbacks, made the dream too large to achieve. Have you ever felt as though you were doing something that seemed completely pointless? I had many visions of being an actor and a pastor while I was in college pursuing a degree in education. I took a semester off after learning to act at Delaware State University to travel with a professional stage play called *My Grandmother Prayed for Me*. I figured I'd made it.

My dreams were off to a fantastic start. I was travelling for free, living in hotels, buying whatever I wanted, and having customized suits made for the shows. The film, however, did not have a long run. The money was misappropriated by family members of the playwright, who handled his affairs, and it was all over in a flash. About a million dollars was embezzled by these individuals. Following that, I returned to school, completed my degree, and began writing stage plays. *When It Rains* is the title of a play I wrote.

When It Rains had a massive debut when it first came out. We played to an audience that was only a few people shy of being completely sold out. Many people gave the play a standing ovation and rave reviews. We set up some dates to perform this play in other parts of Delaware, Maryland, and New Jersey because it seemed like an obvious option. This show was supposed to take me around the United States. Those who were close to the situation thought, as did I, that God was asking us to keep moving forward in faith.

We began engaging with numerous groups of people who seemed to be big-time promoters, and we were inundated with false promises of what they could do for us and where they could lead us. Testimonies of how life-changing the play was poured in each time we performed it. However, several of those performances failed to draw the audiences that the so-called promoters promised. Despite the fact that the show was sponsored by the parents of one of the biggest producers in hip-hop, R&B, gospel, and pop music at the time, the show failed to sell out.

Money was misplaced. Not only was there debt from this production but also from other performances. "Don't worry, the customers will come, the money will come; all you need is the right people to see it," I kept hearing. We took big risks and put our faith in God each time, but the results were unproductive. We became increasingly indebted. I felt as if I were in a desert. Why didn't God provide for us? Why did He let me run out of money and options?

I prayed each time for God to send people from the north, south, east, and west, but they never arrived. Every show gave me renewed hope that the Lord would shower blessings on this show this time, but it wasn't until I was convinced to try it again in New Jersey that it happened. I contacted the theatre in Vineland, New Jersey, and we agreed on a new date for the performance. It didn't look promising for ticket sales right away. I became concerned that more debt would be added and that fewer people would attend the performance.

Yes, I was frightened. To make matters worse, the theatre was experiencing financial difficulties and was on the verge of closing its doors. I ended up having to return to the original location where we had performed the play when we first came to Jersey. I also remembered that I didn't like the numbers that had previously appeared. This was not going to end well. We were in the same spot we'd been in before. However, I had the same reaction as the disciples did when Jesus ordered them to go back out into the deep after they had fished all night in those waters.

Yes, I couldn't believe what I saw the night I performed the play, much as the disciples couldn't believe how many fish they caught at the Lord's command. "What did you see?" you inquire. Oh, no! I just saw a 1400-person sell-out crowd. There were people all over the place. This time, I had a feeling it was going to be different. However, after that, I spoke with a round table of people who, despite the fact that their yes would have convinced an influential community leader to finance the play and tour it extensively, hitchhiked with one another to shoot it down.

Another wealthy person, who had recently appeared in Sylvester Stallone's *Creed* and the upcoming Jamie Foxx film, approached me with an interest in taking the play to the next level. However, someone who was present at the previous roundtable meeting interfered, preventing this consensus from being reached. As a result, I returned to the sterile womb. I became bored and despondent with no other options for making a living as an actor.

I waited around waiting for someone to assign me something. I let people and opposition prevent me from pursuing one of the dreams that God had clearly called me to pursue. Not to mention, things were even more complicated during these hard times because my father, grandmother, and uncle—all of whom were staunch supporters of mine—all went home to be with the Lord. I had a couple of discussions about being the pastor of some existing churches, but none of them came to fruition. And there was the breakup. However, neither my tale nor yours ends in a barren landscape.

I discovered some powerful revelations from my barren womb, which I hope to share with you as you continue to follow your God-sized dream. One thing I discovered during the process is that God will not only make your dreams come true, but He will also make you a dream come true for someone else.

God allows you to go through painful experiences for a reason. Purposeful suffering occurs as God requires you to go through adversity in order to bless others while also maturing you to handle the responsibilities of the dream He has given you. It reminds me of Joseph, Jacob's favorite son, who purposefully went through pain in order to be a blessing to Potiphar's house and, eventually, to preserve Israel. As for the outcome of my purposeful suffering, I am now remarried, I recently appeared on B.E.T.'s latest crime series, *Criminals at Work*, was the lead role in a film, Love and Deceit, and I have launched a new church.

Do you have a God-given dream that seems to be dead? Like your baby is stillborn or your womb is barren? Are you being unproductive? Is it fruitless? Do you feel like you're stuck in a rut, waiting for someone to come along and help you realize your ambitions? Have you ever wondered why God allowed you to become infertile? Do you believe that your dream isn't from God and that your efforts have been in vain? Two extremes occur, which usually assist you in determining whether or not your dream is from God.

First and foremost, you will become enthralled by your dream. Number two, by the way, is that you will be terrified of your dream. A God-given dream can always lead you to unexpected and ironic locations. You're excited about your dream because you're passionate about it and enjoy it. It's the kind of dream you'd have if you never got paid to do it but did it so well that people were willing to pay you for it. Yet, because of the obligation and transparency it entails, you are afraid of it. You're afraid of failing. It's the kind of dream that once you start, you can't stop.

These two extremes remind me of a married pregnant woman. She is ecstatic to learn that she is expecting a child. She goes around informing her family, friends, and co-workers that she is expecting a child and describes how it feels to be pregnant at various stages. She's overjoyed to be pregnant ... until she goes into labor! She's terrified now that she's in labor. She is terrified of the excruciating pain she is experiencing. She's afraid she'll die in the process. *I'm worried the baby will die. I'm worried that something will go wrong with the boy.*

She's in so much agony that she's crying, screaming, and pleading for an epidural, a cesarean section, or something else that can help her get that baby out. I believe God has placed a dream—your son—on the inside of you, just as He has placed a dream on the inside of this pregnant woman. You can say if your dream is from God if you are both excited and scared of it at the same time. Many dreamers have been defeated because they were afraid, not because they had failed. Countless people are prevented from achieving their goals by fear alone.

Nonetheless, you, God's man and woman, make a critical decision today. Do you want to choose between your comfort zone and your dream? You can't have it all. "If it's big enough to scare you, it's God's will for your life," I say all the time. Your dream should be so huge that it provides a work for your faith. Until you give your faith a job, it is unemployed. Until you give it something to believe in and work for.

Blind Bartimaeus cried out for vision after seeing a dream. Blind Bartimaeus was begging on the side of the road when he saw Jesus approaching. He began pleading with Jesus to have mercy on him. Despite several attempts to silence him, he continued to scream even louder. Jesus made his dream of seeing come true as a result of his unwavering confidence. It's worth noting that I said "persevering confidence." The word sever is associated with the word perseverance. Breaking off from a bond or partnership is referred to as severing.

Sometimes, in order to fulfill your dreams, you must first end some meaningless relationships that aren't bringing you any closer to your goals. At this time, I will advise you to examine all of your relationships and bring them through the question mark, comma, and duration phases. To begin, mark all relationships with a question mark. This relationship is up for review to assess what I'm giving and receiving as well as what I need from it spiritually, mentally, emotionally, psychologically, and socially, as shown by a question mark.

A comma in a relationship indicates that you have agreed to take a break from the action in order to renegotiate the terms of the relationship and what you require now is likely to be somewhat different from what you required previously. Finally, a duration indicates that the relationship should be ended. It's not going anywhere anytime soon. It's not good for my well-being, and it's not positive in my life. After that, begin to form bonds with other dreamers who are pregnant and further along than you are. I'll come back to this stage later. Do you think it's weird that your dream might cause any of your family members to be disturbed? Many dreamers become barren as a result of allowing family and friends to talk ill of them.

Enable no one to hold you awake during this time of your life only because they haven't imagined your dream. Understand that God-sized dreams attract haters who will want to destroy your life. Here's the thing: God never said we can just expect good days. John 16:33 says, "I have told you these things, so that in me you may have peace. In this world, you will have trouble. But take heart! I have overcome the world."

The Word of God teaches us to expect trouble as well as good, but don't worry about your trouble because God has overcome the world. I want to encourage every dreamer reading to **LIVE OUT YOUR DREAMS** and let you know that your barren days are over. Isaiah 54:1 says, "'Sing, O barren woman, you who never bore a child; burst into song, shout for joy, you who were never in labor; because more are the children of the desolate woman than of her who has a husband,' says the LORD."

What I learned from my barrenness was that when God is preparing to do something significant in the world, He always does so from a barren womb. Allow me to demonstrate. God created a son in Adam in the beginning, but when He decided to make a son of promise, He used Sarah's womb. Sarah's womb was aged and sterile. When God opened up her womb and she gave birth to Isaac, she was about 91 years old. Rebecah, in exchange, married Isaac. Rebecah, on the other hand, had a problem: she, too, was barren. But because God wanted to do something wonderful in the world, He opened her womb, and Jacob was born from barrenness.

God changed Jacob's name and he had 12 sons, who became the nation of Israel's 12 tribes. Nonetheless, Jacob married the woman of his dreams after marrying the trick—that is the trick that Laban played on him by offering him Leah to marry first. Jacob married Leah and became one with Rachel, his true love. Something is wrong with Rachel, according to the elite motif. She is, therefore, barren. Nonetheless, God desired to do something wonderful on Earth, so He opened her womb, and Joseph emerged. Joseph wasn't just any man; he was destined to become Israel's preserver by God's plan. If I continued, I would tell you about Hannah and Peninnah, who were married to the same guy, Elkanah, as Leah and Rachel were.

Elkanah and Peninnah were having babies all over the place, but his heart belonged to Hannah, as you would imagine. You can probably guess where I'm going at this point. Hannah was barren. Regardless, God desired to do something wonderful on the earth and fulfill someone's dream, so He opened Hannah's womb, and Samuel emerged as one of the greatest prophets and leaders the world has ever known. The story of Elizabeth and Zechariah can be found in the New Testament. According to the Bible, Elizabeth was barren and aged, and she felt like a shame.

Nonetheless, God's miraculous force opened Elizabeth's womb, and from it came John the Baptist, who would go on to become a strong prophet of God and the forerunner of Jesus Christ. I especially like what Elizabeth said about her dream when she was five months pregnant. "The Lord has done this for me," she said in Luke 1:25. To put it another way, she gave God credit for what He was about to accomplish through her. Four months later, she gave birth to a son who would bear her name for the rest of his life.

This is a powerful revelation because it tells us that if we give God credit for what is going on in our lives, He will put it in our names. You may be praying right now for a home, a family, money, and a vehicle to aid you in your ministry. If you start giving God credit for it ahead of time, I believe He will put it in your name. Last but not least, God, who delights in outshining Himself, chose a young virgin named Mary. Mary was the most barren of them all because she had never had sexual relations with a man, but God opened up this virgin womb, and out of it came the greatest man who ever lived.

Jesus was his name. I believe that whenever God wishes to accomplish something significant on Earth, He frequently employs someone with a barren womb. Not only physical but also spiritual wombs are barren. People who have reached a point in their lives where they are unproductive, unfruitful, dry, deserted, and unstimulated. Perhaps you've arrived at a dead end. So relax, because God is about to bring something wonderful into the world, and it will come from your womb.

I believe God has just imbued you with dreams, visions, ideas, and concepts for you to birth in this season. Ephesians 3:1, says, "Now glory is to God, who by his mighty power at work in us can do far more than we would ever dare to ask or even dream of–infinitely beyond our highest prayers, desires, thoughts, or hopes." What I want you to see is that when God is through with your dream, it will be so huge that you won't remember it. *How is this going to happen?* you may be thinking right now. "How is this possible? How can I know?" says the narrator. When Mary asked the same question, the angel said something to her that I like. "The Holy Spirit will come on you, and the glory of the Highest will overwhelm you," the angel replied. "Even in her old age, your relative will have a boy, and she who was said to be unable to conceive is now in her sixth month."

Let's put this solution to work on your questions now. First and foremost, the Holy Spirit will descend upon you and surround you. What does this convey to you? This means that God will never give you a task that you can complete without His help.

You need the Holy Spirit to lead, guide, and fill your life in order to go from barren to blessed. "Your cousin Elizabeth is six months pregnant," the angel said. "What does Elizabeth's pregnancy have to do with Mary's pregnancy?" (Paraphrased) "What does this have to do with my dreams?" I'm glad you inquired. When you're pregnant with a dream, a vision, an idea, or a philosophy, the realization is that you should start hanging out with other pregnant people.

Other visionaries and dreamers avoid dream killers, dream stealers, and dream abortionists by surrounding themselves with dream pushers, dream encouragers, and other dream chasers. Remove yourself from organizations that exist just to convince you that whatever you're trying to do is impossible. What I've realized from my desolate position is that when people tell me no, it doesn't mean I won't be able to achieve my dream; it simply means I won't be able to do so with them.

Barren places will expose the difference between good and unsuccessful people if you pay attention. People who are good are those who want to do what unsuccessful people have told them they can't do. Elizabeth was overflowing with the Holy Spirit and the baby in her womb leaped the moment Mary entered her home and welcomed her. So, what exactly am I saying? This is the hour, dreamer, when you must only associate with people who will cause the baby inside you to leap.

We also know that Elizabeth was six months pregnant at the time Mary became pregnant. What does this mean in terms of my fantasy? This means you can not only associate with other pregnant women but also with others who are more seasoned and further along than you are. People with experience can assist you in getting through the morning sickness of your dreams and visions. As a side note, I find it fascinating that John the Baptist, in his "subconscious" state, leaped inside the womb when Jesus approached.

However, when John the Baptist was fully grown, imprisoned, and learned about Jesus' actions, he sent his disciples to ask Jesus if He was the Savior or if they should expect anyone else. Listen up, dreamers: don't let your ego talk you out of pursuing your God-given goals. God has already given you the victory. Allowing your humanity to talk louder than the spirit inside you when you reach a desolate place in your life is a mistake. Your flesh aspires to be God and to direct your dreams.

Your flesh still tries to affix a fake voice to your subconscious. Cast down the voice if it is producing a fearful spirit. Determine what God's creative mind is and what the enemy's creative mind is. Your dream is limited, not because of God's spoken Word but because of your lack of faith in Him. What God can do in your life is limitless. Your fantasies are becoming a reality. They are yours now and always. Now is the time to claim your inheritance. Similarly, some of you reading this have a desire to see yourself succeed in life and believe that you are destined for greatness. I'd like to remind you that this is not the time to relax. Now is not the time to unwind.

I'm aware that you're progressing, becoming more competitive and well-known. People are beginning to appreciate you and respect your bravery and determination. Some people dislike you, but it's just because you're on the rise. Allowing yourself to get trapped and remaining on the plane you are actually on is not a good idea. Your dream's grandeur necessitates the use of a connecting flight. Your next flight is leaving in a few minutes.

You've been through hurricanes before, so don't let the turbulence of a low-altitude flight deter you from fulfilling your destiny. Think of the individual and life of David, if there was ever a Bible dreamer who knew what it was like to take connecting flights into his purpose and destiny, it was him.

David, a lowly shepherd, was unexpectedly called from the fields where he tended sheep and anointed to be king in a position where he arrived late for the party in one chapter of his life. The fact that the guests couldn't sit and enjoy the celebrations before David arrived is intriguing. Can I add that people are waiting for you to show up and step into the roles that GOD has given you? It's also worth noting that, with the exception of David, everyone arrived at the party clean.

He was filthy when he arrived. The one who had a speck of dirt on him was anointed as king. This, I believe, is to remind us that as we approach God, we must always come as we are and let Him clean us up. After all, we serve a GOD who, before anything else, was a gardener, and a gardener is a person who works in the soil. GOD, the gardener, will take the dirt in your life and turn it into something beautiful.

Have you ever had the sensation of being dirt? Dirt is something that children enjoy playing in. Have you ever felt as though you were being played with by a child? Have you ever played with your heart and emotions? When people come in from outside, they generally wash their hands to remove any dirt. Have you ever felt as if people were washing their hands of you? They assumed you were dead and abandoned you. They thought you'd never improve or get out of your situation. Animals walk on a lot of dirt.

Have you ever felt as if people trampled on you like vicious animals? If you answered yes, you understand what it's like to be filthy like David.

David did not take a non-stop flight to the castle after receiving the distinction of being anointed as Israel's next king and after partying all night. David is not on the throne the next time we read about him; instead, he is out in the field tending his father's sheep the next day.

He does not ascend to the throne, establish a corporation, or establish a church right away. David will have to wait another 15 years or more to become king. When GOD gives you a dream or anoints you for something significant, it is frequently for a later period. Yet, GOD begins to put you through a process and on a flight to develop the character you will need for the position He has called you to fill. In the very next chapter of David's life, while he's tending sheep, he is summoned from the field again by his father.

His aunt, Jesse, told him to go down to the battlefield and feed three of his brothers who were enlisted in King Saul's army. David immediately followed his father's instructions. It was going to be an easy job for David, just a quick stop and drop. He probably didn't want to leave the sheep and wished he could stay with them. I'm sure he had no idea at the time that this small mission would turn into a massive connecting flight to his destination.

David set out on a mission to feed his older brothers, dressed in a sheep-herder's uniform. He arrived on the battlefield looking like a fish out of water. Everyone on the island had been outfitted, prepared, and equipped with the resources and skills necessary to wage battle, kill, and destroy. King Saul's army was stationed on one mountain, while the Philistine army was stationed on another, ready to strike. David, on the other hand, arrived with a bag of food for his brothers and their commander, despite his lack of training, ability, equipment, and experience. Goliath, the Philistines' giant champion, had dared every brave soldier in Saul's army to come and battle him, but no one would come forward.

Goliath, the mighty warrior, terrified Saul's army. As many of you know, little unafraid David volunteered to fight this uncircumcised Philistine and was quickly recruited into a leadership role. God has a way of placing into positions of power people who are unqualified, disqualified, do not meet the criteria, uneducated, disadvantaged, and untamed in order to perplex the wise.

He uses those who are at their lowest, in the belly of a shark, who have just recently repented, to offer a message of repentance. He loves to use ex-cons, ex-addicts, and divorced people who feel insecure and like failures; people who believe they've made too many mistakes in life to succeed. God likes to use people who can confidently and unashamedly say, "If it hadn't been for the Lord, who was on my side, where would I be?" People who can never take credit for their accomplishments and instead say, "This is the Lord's doing, and it is wonderful in our eyes."

David was taking and serving his brothers lunch on his connecting flight to his kingdom assignment. He would have lost his chance to be king if he had missed his connecting flight as a delivery boy. Don't miss the plane that will take you to the kingdom trip you've always wanted to take. You've been chosen to fly on connecting flights. You might have to sit next to someone whose breath stinks or smells like alcohol, but make sure you don't miss your connecting flight.

You will have to sprint through the airport to catch the next flight, but make sure you don't miss it. Don't miss your flight if you have to deal with the fear of turbulent winds, the discomfort of rising and falling, the stress of the journey, or the layover. So many of us miss out on our dreams because our flights aren't nonstop and mostly take us to places we don't want to go or didn't plan on visiting. Connecting flights can also place you in awkward or uncomfortable circumstances. It was discouraging to learn that I would not be welcomed back to my teaching job. It was a bad experience. Despite the fact that my wife had a good career, the house mortgage wasn't too high at the time, and my car was paid in full, it was always a frightening time for me. After all, I've always assumed that a man's role in his home should be that of priest, defender, pursuer, and provider.

God gave the man work before he was given a woman, I learned. I was told that a man who cannot look after his family is worse than an infidel. Throughout the summer, I applied to a variety of schools in search of a new teaching position. One school called me early in the summer and asked me to come in for an interview. This particular school adored me and was eager to recruit me as soon as possible. However, there were a few issues with this chance, in my opinion.

The first issue was that this school was open all year, which meant that I would have to return to work the next day after being employed. I was looking forward to my summer as a hardworking teacher, coach, and pastor of a growing church. I use the summer to read, refresh, and regroup in preparation for the next group of students I'll be teaching. Furthermore, the school was an hour's drive from my home. Third, the pay was a major source of dissatisfaction for me.

This teaching job paid marginally less than what I was already earning at a school that was just seven minutes away and didn't need me to work during the summer. I initially said yes to this school out of fear of missing a pay day. However, after a long and difficult discussion with my God, myself, and my mom, I made the difficult decision to revoke my yes and place my faith in God for greater things. An overshadowing sense of calm seemed to consume me as soon as I shifted my attention away from my circumstances and back to God.

I started to believe in the process. After that, I never had to worry about finding work again. During that time of crisis, my wife and I never stopped tithing or giving. During that time, I believe we gave a little more, and it felt good. During this period of crisis in my life, I discovered that gaining momentum and being on the rise share a few characteristics. They both have a meaning that means growing in popularity and achievement. On the other hand, in order to achieve momentum, such as on a flying trapeze or a pendulum, and to climb higher, you can need to suffer a loss in order to prepare yourself to go higher or faster.

A high jumper can take a step back to get a head start in order to jump higher. To gain enough momentum for lift-off, a plane will start backwards. Similarly, it is not unusual to first encounter a loss or crisis in your life before gaining traction and being on the rise. It was being fired from a job that had become all too familiar and comfortable for me. I would have turned a temporary situation into a permanent one if I hadn't been relieved of my duties.

God knew I'd never leave that job on my own to find anything better, so He had to make that employer reject me. Rejection is frequently a tool that God employs to get you out of a situation that He never intended for you to be in or remain in forever. He uses rejection to His advantage. It's past time for you to change your mind about it. Don't just put up with rejection; welcome it as God's way of getting you off a ship that He doesn't want you to sink trying to stay on.

David, too, felt rejected and dejected on his connecting flight. He was on the up and up. He was gaining popularity among the populace. He was gathering strength as a result of his war victories. "Saul has slain his thousands, and David has slain his tens of thousands," the women sang as they danced. These chants infuriated King Saul, and he was afraid that the people who elected him would ultimately want David to be king, so he set out on a course to kill David.

David was rejected not only by his king, who represents his authority, but also by his father and daughters, who represent his relationships. He lost his relationships and power during his crisis of being on the run from his king. To survive, David had to abandon his home, his wife, his best friend, his work, and his city. Merab, the king's daughter, who was supposed to be David's wife, was given to another man when he was on the run. His situation had deteriorated to the point that the only job he could find was fighting for his foes. Because of the Philistines' distrust of David, he did such a good job fighting for his enemies that they gave him the keys to the city of Ziklag.

David and his mighty men were once again on the rise, marrying, having children, and starting families. Even the temporary circumstance, though, did not turn out well. As they returned home from battle, they found Ziklag in flames, burning to the ground, and that the Amalekites had taken all of their women and children. David felt the stinging pain of rejection and dejection again at this stage, for not only had his wives been taken, but his mighty men now wanted to stone him to death because their families had been taken as well.

David felt like the world's greatest disappointment. He seemed to be too far removed from the events that had been predicted for his existence. He probably felt that he couldn't get much further removed from the king he was anointed to be. But he was never so near. David persuaded himself in the Lord and debated with God about what to try after all he had lost.

He and his mighty men ended up crushing the Amalekites, recovering all of their families, and gathering such a lot of spoils that they blessed the elders in Judah with the plunder they had recovered. Before he could enjoy his family and the spoils of victory, David got news that King Saul and David's best friend Jonathan were dead. It was a bittersweet moment in David's life. Knowing that King Saul and Jonathan were dead was bitter to chew, but his intent and destiny were sweeter than honey.

God told David that he should take another connecting flight to Judah, and David agreed. The fact that David's city, Ziklag, had been burned down also helped. David, his family, and his men and their families all arrived in Hebron right away. In Hebron, David, who had been a colossal disappointment in Ziklag, became a success story. He wasn't yet the king of all of Israel, but he was on the rise in Hebron. He began to gain traction in Hebron. His wives were also restored to him in Hebron, and new wives were given to him.

Maakah was one of the wives worth mentioning. She was the daughter of Geshur's king, Talmai. David wouldn't be able to marry her until he was king. To put it another way, he couldn't marry her until he got to her level and ascended to her status. In essence, Maakah gave David what he could have gotten from Merab, King Saul's daughter, who was supposed to be given to him but instead went to another man. As you accept your season of connecting flights, I believe God will begin to restore everything that was taken from you and given to someone else.

Also, I believe God will restore your relationships and rebuild your homes that were destroyed when you were fighting to save someone else's home. In the end, I felt like my previous school had been burned down like Ziklag. I felt like I'd failed miserably. I had no idea I was on the upswing. Despite everything, I learned that sometimes, in order for you to get on the right track or a better track, God has to derail you from the one you're currently on.

I had a great time during my summer vacation. I was able to spend quality time with my family, travel with my sons for their AAU basketball endeavors, advise and transport men who were addicted to drugs to inpatient services, and be fully accessible to my church's members. However, just a few days before the new school year began, I began to receive several phone calls inviting me to come in for interviews for teaching positions that I had applied for at the end of the previous school year. I received many work offers from the schools for which I interviewed the week before school started.

One of the deals was for $12,000 more than I had earned at my previous job. If that wasn't enough, the following week I received another offer from a school, this time for $15,000 more per year than I had previously earned. To top it off, the most recent interview I had attended gave me a $22,000 raise over my previous salary. I chose and accepted the teaching role that was 10 minutes away from my previous house and ministry because of my family and the ministry God has called me to. Of course, this job even had summers off.

The fact that my salary was never deducted from my account astounded me. When I received my first check from my new job, I received my last paycheck from my former employer. The fact is if I hadn't taken that connecting flight, I wouldn't have been prepared for my fate on the flight I'm actually on. The connecting flight gave me the opportunity to obtain all of the certifications I'd need to fly on this particular flight. God allowed me to get married, start a ministry, take some free courses toward my master's degree, and so much more while on my connecting flight.

If you want to be a rising dreamer, you'll need to learn how to handle connecting flights. The path to your dream will most likely consist of a series of flights linking you to your destiny rather than a single nonstop flight to the throne. I only wanted to make sure you didn't miss your connecting flight or you'd end up sitting on the bay's dock, observing the tide recede.

God is about to place you on the same plane as people who are twice your age, twice your skill level, and twice your equipment, yet this is not a time to become intimidated by them but a time for you to become motivated. The person of your dreams is waiting. Wealth is waiting. Not just you, but everybody that's connected to you will receive the benefits you're getting. Do not see your connecting flight as an obstacle but as an opportunity to rise higher and go further than you've ever gone.

PRINCIPLE POINTS

◆ Your dream is your direction; all the information and every instruction and direction you need is in your dream.

◆ When God talks to us through dreams, we must do some work in order to be led by a clear vision.

◆ A simple dream guided every great leader in the Bible.

◆ Sometimes, to fulfill your dreams, you must end some meaningless relationships that aren't bringing you any closer to your goals.

CHAPTER 5

DESIGNED TO DREAM

What do Abraham, Jacob, Joseph, Caleb, and Solomon, among other biblical figures, have in common with God? They were determined dreamers as well as great men of faith. God was a dreamer until He became a provider, healer, and ever-present aid in times of need. He is a never-ending dreamer. The Bible, his novel, is full of God's dreams come true.

One of His greatest ambitions was to have a family of sons and daughters with whom he could share His power and dominion. As a result, He created us in His image and likeness, imbuing us with not only the power to reproduce but also His incredible desire to dream. We are, in a way, God's dream team. Merriam Webster defines a dream as:

1. A series of thoughts, images, or emotions.

2. A strongly desired goal or purpose.

We can see from this meaning that God has given us the same essence as Him, which includes deep longings, intense desires, and visions. We were made to dream. And if He has given us the opportunity to dream, there must be a way to make them come true. Our meaning comes from achieving our God-given goals. You must first obey God with your entire heart if you are to fulfill your dreams and visions from Him and take possession of His promises. You can't just go along for the ride half-heartedly. God expects you to put something into it.

Caleb was blessed with the land of his dreams, Hebron, according to the Bible, which says three times in Joshua 14 that he was blessed because he wholeheartedly embraced the Lord, the God of Israel. The Bible is more than a book of rules and laws; it is a book of dreams and power principles or cheat codes to accomplishing our dreams as well.

Dream It

To begin with, your dreams should be so large that they put your confidence to work. Until you give your faith something significant to believe God for, it is dormant. It is not a dream from God if you can achieve your goals on your own, without the assistance of God. God would never grant you a life vision that you can achieve without His help. Not only that, but a God-sized dream is one that God bestows on you and to which He adds His own dream. That is what makes your ambition so lofty.

God gave Abram a dream in Genesis 12:1–3. He promised Abram that He would make him a great country, that He would bless him, that He would make his name great, that He would make him a blessing, that He would bless those who bless Abram, and that He would curse those who curse him. God shared and associated His dream with Abram's dream as He gave it to Abram. "And by you, all the inhabitants of the earth will be blessed," God said. God's dream was of how He would bless the earth, and it was through Abram's dream that He would do so. God changed Abram's dream from personal achievement to meaning in that one moment.

God-sized dreams are about more than just making your name famous; they're about making a big difference in other people's lives. I'm curious what would happen if you extended your thought process about your visions and desires to include God's dreams. To be honest, I believe you will see that God has placed a dream on your heart that has the power to bless the entire world.

That's incredible! Never restrict yourself because of the limitations of someone else's imagination. Enable no one to keep you awake only because they haven't had the same dreams as you. Abram's God-given dream would eventually lead to the birth of the world's Savior, Jesus. In other words, Abram's dream from God brought him salvation. Dreams have the ability to save lives. Jacob's beloved son— Joseph—his dream saved a nation. God's dream saved the world. Imagine how many can be saved by you fulfilling your God-given dream.

Desire It

If you want to take your dreams to the next level, achieve success, and have a significant impact, you must first have a strong desire for them. It's not as easy as wishing upon a star for it to happen. You won't be able to put on a magical mask or be bitten by a spider and gain superpowers all of a sudden. It must, however, be a heavy desire and a deep longing. Before any desire, there is a feeling that precedes it.

Proverbs 23:7 says, "For as he thinks in his heart, so is he." French philosopher Rene Descartes said, "I think, therefore I am." In other words, my thoughts fuel my drive to become something I've imagined. So having a burning desire for the dream is the first step in making it a reality. Combine your dream with the confidence that you will achieve it. You must have such a deep conviction in it that you are able to burn all other bridges for it and have no backup plan. I was at a prophetic prayer breakfast on Saturday when the keynote speaker, a strong woman of God, called me out.

She then instructed one of her assistants to deliver some eggs and a basket to me. They put the basket next to me and handed me the eggs. She would randomly glance at me to see if I had received the message as she continued to deliver a powerful phrase. I said no a few times because I didn't understand why this woman had me keeping eggs during the service. Then it dawned on me. God opened my understanding so that I could see that she wanted me to place the eggs in the basket. "It didn't take a rocket scientist to find that out," you're probably saying. Nonetheless, the woman of God wanted me to realize that I will not be able to possess the promise unless I am ready to cut all other ties and throw all of my hopes and dreams into one basket.

I was awestruck because, at that moment, I was treading carefully and dabbling in different opportunities. At that point, I realized that believing entails not only trusting God without knowing how He will resolve the situation but also trusting Him enough to place all of your eggs in one basket. There is no contingency plan in place. There is no backup plan. You've all agreed to participate.

I recently heard a story about a king who decided to conquer and own a new land that he had discovered. As a result, he and all of his soldiers sailed to this new territory. When they landed, he demanded that all of the ships be burned. "Either we conquer this land or we die," he told his army.

Needless to say, they were successful in conquering the nation. The argument is that desire must be at the core of any God-given dream, and it must be combined with faith that what you are yearning for is God's plan for your life. According to Psalm 27:4, King David said, "One thing have I desired of the Lord, that will I seek after..." Notice, he did not pursue a slew of fantasies. He just pursued one. What is the one burning wish you've had for a long time? What is the one goal that, if achieved, will completely change your life? The one vision that, if you followed it, would gain so many souls? Stop snoozing your wishes because they are God's way of communicating with you.

God communicates with us not only through angels, visions, the Holy Spirit, promptings, and His name but also through our desires. Psalm 37:4 says, "Delight yourself in the Lord and he will give you the desires of your heart." When you delight in God, He interacts with you through your wishes. Second, impulses will lead to the creation of action plans, which is when innovation will begin. Let us look at God's example in this regard. God had a vision, devised an action plan, and then started to create. To put it another way, imagination does not occur without the presence of a fantasy.

In Jeremiah 1:5, God says, "Before I formed you in the womb I knew you before you were born I set you apart." The word knew is the Hebrew word "yada," which means to intimately see; to perceive, and be well acquainted with. God was saying that not only did He have a reoccurring dream about Jeremiah, but He also developed a game plan for his life before He created him. Psalm 139:16 says, "Your eyes saw my unformed body; all the days ordained for me were written in your book before one of them came to be." This text is suggesting God had a dream of us, wrote the vision for our lives, and then started the creation process. Hence, creativity does not happen without first having a dream. If you can dream it, God will give you the power to plan and create it.

Dreams Deferred

How you react to a temporary setback will decide how good you are at turning your dreams into reality. In Genesis 1:1–2, the Bible states, "In the beginning, God created the heaven and the earth. And the earth was without form and void, and darkness was upon the face of the deep…" According to biblical scholars who believe in the Gap Theory, God built the universe perfectly in verse one. Verse two, on the other hand, assumes that the universe became unstable, gloomy, and disorderly as a result of a major catastrophic event.

Following that, the plot picks up with the Holy Spirit working to heal and recreate the brokenness. Many of these theories claim that Satan's revolt and collapse caused the chaos. And the world became barren and uninhabitable as a result of God's plan for it. If that wasn't enough, Satan came in and persuaded Adam and Eve to pursue a different agenda after God produced man and woman, His crowning masterpiece, after He gave them authority to be fruitful, multiply, replenish, subdue, and have control, and after God gave them the terms and conditions.

Adam and Eve sinned in the Garden of Eden when they took their gaze away from the dream. God's dream of creating a family was briefly shattered. Satan enjoys sabotaging God's plan. If Satan dared to go after God's dream, I'm sure he's sent and will send giants to go after yours as well. Many of you reading this chapter right now might feel as though the events of the past year have broken your dreams. Keep dreaming and reading this chapter, I encourage you. You'll rekindle your desire to fulfill those shattered dreams. A little over a year ago, the world awoke with trepidation to a day that would go down in history.

The coronavirus Covid-19 pandemic became the world's most serious threat since World War II. It was a worldwide health emergency. Each newspaper had an article about it on the front page. Every news source reported on it. Although Fox News applauded the president's response to the pandemic, CNN, MSNBC, and other news organizations criticized and challenged the president's strategy and decisions. The stock market started to plummet. Government buildings and public schools were shuttered. Events all over the world were postponed.

Shortages and delays were more serious. There were layoffs. Unemployment was at an all-time high. I never imagined a day when churches would shut their doors while liquor stores and marijuana dispensaries remained open. The coronavirus has killed almost three million people, at the time of writing. And, as Paul Lawrence Dunbar famously put it, "we wear the masks."

As if the world pandemic wasn't bad enough, socioeconomic inequality had reached new heights. Racism has a new lease of life. On May 25, 2020, a police officer whose duty it is to protect and serve kneeled for eight minutes and 46 seconds on the neck of George Floyd, an unarmed black man. A modern-day lynching was observed around the world. Floyd's death brought attention to the tragic death of Breonna Taylor, a 26-year-old African American woman. On March 13, 2020, she was also shot and killed in her apartment by white plainclothes police officers. Breonna Taylor's family has yet to receive justice as of this writing.

Yes, we've had some of the worst days we've ever seen, and dreams seem to have been robbed in this season of life. Nonetheless, I urge you to keep dreaming and not give up. Do you realize that we serve a God who understands what it's like to have your hopes shattered? But, in His infinite wisdom, God devised a scheme to bring His dreams back to life before the problem arose.

That's why Jesus is referred to in Revelation 13:8 as "the Lamb who was slain from the beginning of the earth." That is, God had a solution before the problem even existed. And the good news is that He has a mission to bring your dreams back to life as well. When God is about to do something different, it is always preceded by darkness, according to the Dream-giver's book. To put it another way, darkness is a sign that God is working behind the scenes. The Bible says that after the world became formless and empty, and darkness fell upon the face of the deep, God's Spirit began to move and regenerate.

The Spirit's movement was preceded by darkness. Similarly, the Bible says that darkness fell over the whole universe at the sixth hour, or around noon, when Jesus was dying on the cross. Jesus was crucified, buried, and then raised from the dead. When God does something different, it is often accompanied by darkness. If your dreams have been broken by the past year of darkness, realize that God has planned a greater dream for you through that darkness.

God knows how to take away the power of evil to kill. Dutch Sheets tells a story about a magnificent and valuable mosaic at Tehran's royal palace in his book *Dream*. Originally, the mosaic's designer intended to use large sheets of mirror to decorate the palace walls. The contractor found the mirrors were all smashed and broken into pieces when the shipments arrived. The builder had a stroke of brilliance as he summoned the contractor to collect all of the shattered glass.

The builder then shattered the broken bits into tiny fragments and stuck them to the palace's walls. The architect stunned everyone when he transformed a shattered glass into a dazzling mosaic. God is the great architect of our hopes and dreams. Jeremiah 29:11 tells us He knows the plans that He has for us. Plans to give us hope and a future. He sees what we can become, not just what we are. We must learn to place our confidence in Him. God delights in taking beauty out of ashes and making mosaics out of shattered glass. Keep dreaming if you're currently broken. Pray and ask God to make a mosaic out of your messes.

I love how Job 14:7–9 states, "Even a tree has more hope! If it is cut down, it will sprout again and grow new branches… yet at the scent of water it will bud and put out branches like a young plant." When you feel like your dreams have been shattered and cut down, all you have to do is surround yourself with people who smell like dreamers and watch your dreams bloom once more. Get around someone pregnant, like Mary and Elizabeth did, and watch the baby God has given you leap and live again.

Decide It

Many people struggle to fulfill their God-given aspirations because they allow procrastination to take over due to their unwillingness to make a decision and follow through. I want you to affirm these words as you pursue your dreams this year:

• "I'll make a fast decision and then slowly change my mind."

• "On the Holy Spirit's urging, I will share my vision with others."

Since he knows that certain people are anointed in talking us out of every word God has spoken over our lives, James advises us to be fast to listen and slow to speak. They'll shape committees just to tell you it's impossible and it's not your season. Giving in to these negative voices will cause you to pause only long enough to miss an opportunity. We must recognize that God is in motion. When the world was filled with darkness, the Holy Spirit moved quickly to intervene and do something about it.

Throughout the Old Covenant, God's people were led by the cloud by day and the fire by night. We see Jesus moving quickly and directly in the New Covenant. Paul backs up his claim by saying, "For those who are guided by the spirit of God are God's children." In the last chapter of Revelation, Jesus said, "Surely I come quickly..." To put plainly, God is a quick-moving God who does not waste time waiting for someone. Simply procrastinating will cause you to drift away from Him and fall short of His glory. Backsliding occurs not because you reverted to a sin from which you had been delivered but because you remained still while God moved on.

When God gives you a dream, you must act quickly to make it a reality, which means making a fast decision and taking immediate action. I believe that if you pursue your dreams with renewed zeal this season, God will make your dreams a reality in front of everyone who said it wasn't your time.

Declare It

The ability to decree and announce is one of the most powerful resources God has given us in our pursuit of our dreams. Elijah prayed for rain and then prayed for it not to rain. And all of these things came to pass. To put it another way, he had the ability to talk a season into and out of his life. Similarly, you have the authority to talk about those opportunities that come your way. "God has given you the power to talk a funeral or a future," someone once said. I'm referring to confidence.

In Romans 10:17, Paul says, "So then faith comes by hearing, and hearing by the word of God." You must, strictly speaking, speak the Word of God or make affirmations over dreams on a regular basis. You must announce them to the extent that you think you have what you're announcing already. It has already been completed in the Spirit. The reality is that it is already the case. Ephesians 1:3 "confirms that we are blessed with all spiritual blessings in heavenly places." This is why Jesus said, "Believe that you have got it when you wish, and it will be yours." When you make regular faith affirmations over your life, your mind will begin to function on the thoughts you want it to and work hard to bring them to fruition.

To be honest, no matter what you say, if your affirmations are not backed by faith in God, they will not work for you. "These people worship me with their mouths, and honour me with their tongues, but their hearts are far from me," God says in Isaiah 29:13. They adore me, but it's all for naught. Simply put, lip service isn't enough if you don't have confidence. In your effort to pursue your God-given dream, you must dream it, desire it, decide on it quickly, declare it, and lastly discern it.

Discern It

To detect is to see; to perceive with one's eyes, ears, or other senses, or with one's intellect; to comprehend. To put it another way, discernment entails having a vision. "Eyes that look are normal, but eyes that can see are rare," Myles Munroe said. Vision creates action plans on what you want to do. "I will stand at my guard post and station myself on the ramparts," Habakkuk 2:1 said. I'll be watching to see what He says to me and how I can react if I'm corrected." What's noteworthy about this passage is the prophet's statement that he will "wait" and "see" what God will say.

The one issue we see in the text is that we normally don't use our eyes to see what someone is doing while we're waiting for them to say something. For the most part, we use our ears to hear what someone is thinking. I assume his statement contains a secret fact. The truth is that if God speaks to us, we must translate what He says into something we can picture in our minds. That, I believe, is why Habakkuk says in the second verse, "Write the vision." Notice that he didn't say,

"Write what you heard me say," but rather, "Write what you saw while I was speaking."

Make a list of what you dreamed. You must be a visionary if you want to pursue your God-given dreams. A visionary sees meaning above money and performance. Visionaries see beyond the present to the future. Not only did Jesus see fishermen, but he also saw disciples. In Mary of Magdala, he saw a preacher and a follower, not a prostitute. Christ saw more than sinners in us; he saw a bride. Be sure to write down your vision as clearly as possible. Even if it appears unbelievable to you and others, include everything you dreamed when God shared it with you.

This is not the time to restrict yourself due to the limitations of someone else's imagination. To say it another way, do not allow people to keep you asleep just because they haven't dreamed what you dreamt. You are the only person who has a balcony view of your vision. Everyone else only has a basement view. Proverbs 29 first 18 states, "Where there is no vision the people perish." It didn't say where there isn't a husband or wife, house or car, family, or church. Where there is no vision, the Word is spoken.

To put it another way, either you will dream or you will die, perhaps not a literal death but definitely a figurative one. The Hebrew word for perish is "para," which means "without restriction." People are unrestrained where there is no vision. When you look at trees in the forest that are growing without restriction, you'll notice that they compete every day of their lives. They are always trying to out-position the other trees in order to get some of the sunlight they need to rise and tower over them.

People without a goal, on the other hand, will still be competing with others and politicking for roles and titles. Perish may also refer to anything that is out of reach, such as a vehicle without brakes. People who lack vision are out of control and on the verge of self-destruction. They are untethered, which means they go rogue. Those with vision, on the other hand, are in command, on their way to success, self-disciplined, and aware of who they are. An individual who has good vision will not be disturbed.

He won't waste time working in a profession that doesn't align with his goals. She isn't going to waste her time in a relationship with a guy who isn't capable of covering her. It's a pleasure to be around someone who has vision. I announce that when you apply these life-changing concepts to your dreams, God will shower you with more visions and dreams. I announce that He is giving you a vision that is multiplied. You're about to have a wild dream.

In this season, don't be surprised if your dreams annoy any family members. Your dreams are causing God to make you extraordinary. He is about to render you visible because you've been invisible for far too long. You'll be the next one to bear witness. Your dreams are about to cure you in every place where you've been suffering and missing. Finally, I declare and decree that God will use your dreams to help Him realize His dreams and bless a generation.

PRINCIPLE POINTS

◆ It is not a dream from God if you can achieve your goals on your own.

◆ You're designed to dream, but you need to work it out.

◆ To make your dream a reality, you need to:
- Dream It
- Desire It
- Decide It
- Declare It
- Discern It

CONCLUSION

God speaks …

God has amazing plans for our lives. He created us to have goals and dreams, to continually reach for more in our life in Christ. When God gives you a dream, it's like becoming pregnant: you conceive (think or imagine) a vision or idea of the "new thing" He's planned for you. Then, after conception, you go through a season of "pregnancy"—a time of growth and preparation for your dream to become reality.

In the beginning, when you're making plans to live out your dream, it's exciting and easy to be enthusiastic about the process. But those emotions can't be the driving force of your determination because they will subside over time. Ecclesiastes 5:3 AMPC says, "For a dream comes with much business and painful effort…"

This is why many people abort their dreams before they reach full-term.

God plants a seed (dream) in them and they become pregnant. But when they find out it will take effort, be costly, inconvenient, or uncomfortable to complete their preparation for the birth, they decide it wasn't God's will after all and go and do something else.

I want to encourage you to go through the hard part because if you give up, you will never be completely satisfied. There will be a part of you that doesn't feel settled or fulfilled. God is a God who dreams and as being made in His likeness, in His image, we should dream too. Otherwise, we put to death Ephesians 3:20 and effectively allow the enemy to yield us powerless in seeing the miracles of God.

Rodney Davis

LEADER

Elder Rodney Davis, husband and father of six, is the pastor of Transformation Church, where his purpose is to pattern the heartbeat of God's people after the heartbeat of God by presenting a Christian paradigm, equipping and motivating men and women who desire to fulfill God's purpose for their lives through the arts, ministry, and education, and providing the practical and spiritual groundwork needed to achieve success and significance.

EDUCATOR

Rodney Davis received his Bachelor of Arts degree from Delaware State University, majoring in English and Music Education. For over 15 years he has worked with students enrolled in adult education programs and alternative schools and is currently working as a kindergarten teacher in the

Capital School District. In 2011, he was named Educator of the Year by the Omega Psi Phi Fraternity, Inc.

You can connect with Rodney via

Web: www.transformationofde.com

Email: Transformationchurchde@yahoo.com

Facebook: @rodney.davis3

Instagram: @pastorrldavis

Twitter: @Roddav

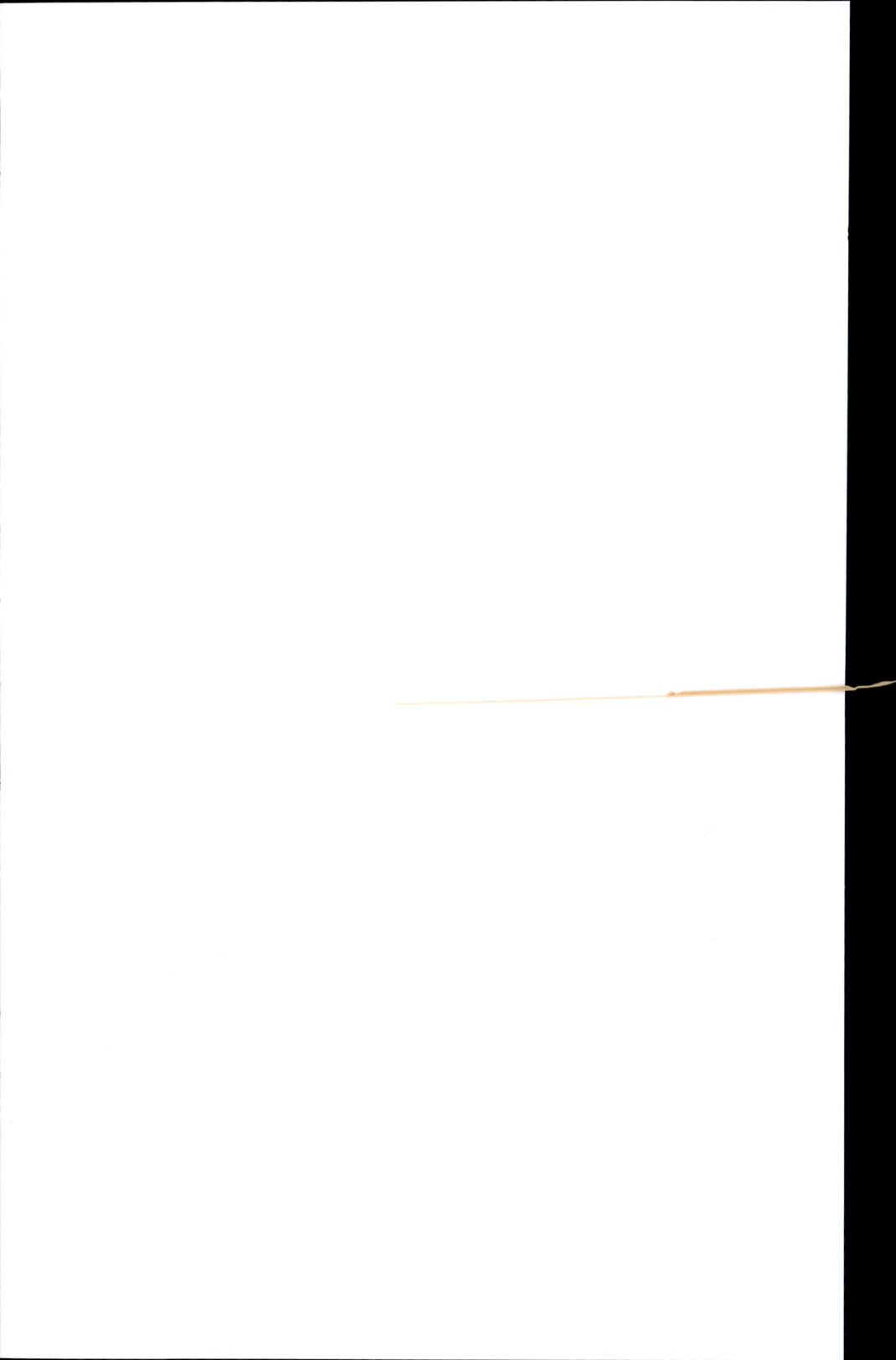

www.ingramcontent.com/pod-product-compliance
Lightning Source LLC
Chambersburg PA
CBHW070540030426
42337CB00016B/2278